Grammaropolis
PRESENTS

Vinny the Action Verb & Lucy the Linking Verb

Written by Coert Voorhees
Illustrations by Powerhouse Animation

Meet the Parts of Speech

I name a specific person, place, thing, or idea. It's a big responsibility, naming things— a responsibility that requires a certain attention to detail.

Nelson the Noun

Some people say I'm all over the place. Some people call me a ball of energy. I take that as a compliment, because I just like to go, go, go!

Vinny the Action Verb

I take the place of one or more Nouns or Pronouns. I always want the Noun's job, and I hang out with the Verb and Adjective.

Roger the Pronoun

I'm perfectly happy to link Nouns and Pronouns with the appropriate Adjectives, but it's not like I'm going to expend a lot of energy doing so.

Lucy the Linking Verb

I modify a Noun or Pronoun. I tell what kind, which one, how many, or how much. I pride myself on being the most artistic of the parts of speech.

Jake the Adjective

Gather 'round everybody and let's have ourselves a wonderful time. I just love bringing words and groups of words together, don't you?

Connie the Conjunction

I modify a Verb, Adjective, or other Adverb. I tell how, when, where, to what extent, and under what condition. I often end in –ly, but I don't have to.

Benny the Adverb

I express emotion!! Yep, I'm always here, always ready with my commas and exclamation points, just in case.

Izzy the Interjection

They call me Preposition because I'm pre-positioned. I'm first. At the front. Before every other word in the phrase? Got it?

Li'l Pete the Preposition

I am a chameleon. A spy. An undercover operative. I infiltrate the sentence and act as whatever part of speech suits me.

Slang

VINNY THE ACTION VERB AND LUCY THE LINKING VERB

© 2019 Grammaropolis

Graphic Design by Mckee Frazior

Text and Illustrations © 2011 by Grammaropolis LLC

This book is typeset in Komika Text

Distributed throughout the world by Ingram Publisher Services www.ingrambook.com

He loved to
jump and fly.

2

Vinny's dream was to express his action as a superhero.

We **are** not superheroes. We **are** verbs. We **=** verbs.

I **will fight** crime!

I **will save** people!

5

Luckily for Vinny, there was a knock at the door. It was Li'l Pete the preposition.

Lucy, on the other hand, worked well with adjectives.
Jake needs us!
Okay, fine.
to be, or
not to be.

Lucy expressed Jake's state of being.
You seem scared.
It's Benny the adverb.

Vinny was worried. He knew the adverb could pick on him, too.

This called for some superhero teamwork. Lucy suggested a state of being.

Hey, Benny. You *seem* hungry.

Somewhat.

22

Being in Action: Verb Notes

An action verb expresses action!

ACTION VERBS

They *enjoy* family time.
Mandy *ate* a pear.
Bill *walked*.

LINKING VERBS

My penguin *is* cold.
That apple *was* red.
She *looks* sad.

A linking verb expresses a state of being.

ACTION VERBS

An action verb expresses mental or physical action. Action verbs can be transitive or intransitive.

I watched a great movie and danced on my way home from the theater. Then I slept all night.

EXAMPLES

watched
danced
slept

TRANSITIVE VERBS

Transitive verbs pass action to an object.

EXAMPLES

Francine **played** basketball.
Shawn **climbed** a mountain.

In those examples, played passes its action to the direct object basketball, and climbed passes its action to the direct object mountain.

INTRANSITIVE VERBS

Intransitive verbs work alone, without objects.

EXAMPLES

Francine danced.

Shawn slept.

In these examples, there are no objects after danced or slept, so the verbs are intransitive.

TRANSITIVE OR INTRANSITIVE?

Some words can be transitive or intransitive, depending on how they're used.

TRANSITIVE

I **ate** a hamburger.

I **ate** WHAT ? A hamburger! So the verb is transitive!

How do you tell?
1. Find the action verb.
2. Ask "what?" after it.
3. If the answer is in the sentence, you've found a transitive verb!!

INTRANSITIVE

I **ate** before Lucy.

I **ate** WHAT ? I certainly didn't eat Lucy, so the answer isn't in the sentence, The verb must be intransitive!

LINKING VERBS

A linking verb expresses a state of being. Linking verbs link the subject of the verb to information that renames or describes the subject. They often take a form of the verb "to be," but they don't have to.

HOT TIP:
If you can replace the verb with = , and the sentence still makes sense, it's a linking verb!

EXAMPLES

My dog is a bundle of joy.   My dog = a bundle of joy.
He looks happy   He = happy

Both make sense! Is and looks are linking verbs!

ACTION VERB OR LINKING VERB?

Some words can be linking verbs or action verbs, depending on the way they're used. How do you know which is which? Here's one way to tell: replace the verb with a form of "to be." If the sentence still makes sense, it was a linking verb all along!

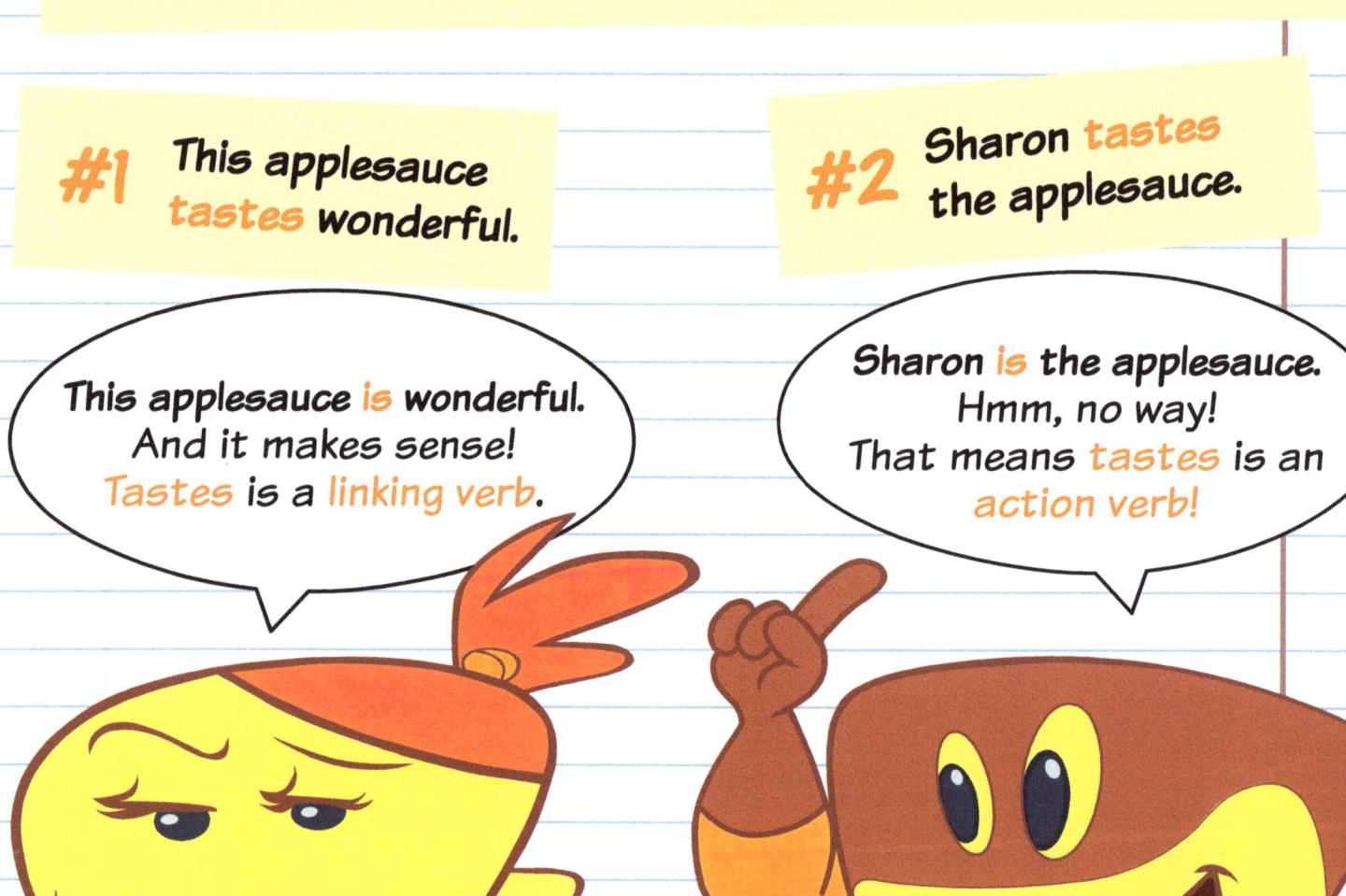

www.ingramcontent.com/pod-product-compliance
Lightning Source LLC
LaVergne TN
LVHW071213200326
834410LV00018B/575